Stories from the Old Testament

Illustrated by Marty Noble

DOVER PUBLICATIONS, INC.
Garden City, New York

Bibliographical Note

Stories from the Old Testament is a new work, first published by Dover Publications, Inc., in 2001.

International Standard Book Number

ISBN-13: 978-0-486-41323-5
ISBN-10: 0-486-41323-3

Manufactured in the United States by LSC Communications
41323311   2021
www.doverpublications.com

NOTE

Down through the centuries, the Bible has been a source of inspiration and instruction for people in many lands. In addition to moral lessons and directives, the Bible has provided readers of all ages with some of the best-loved stories in Western culture.

The stories in this book are based on the Old Testament from the King James version of the Bible. Beginning with the creation of Adam and Eve, they recount the story of humankind, their trials and tribulations, triumphs and transcendence over adversity. Replete with adventure, mystery, miraculous happenings, and the wisdom and folly of people down through the ages, these enduringly popular narratives retain a special power to enrich the lives of all who come to them, generation after generation.

We hope you enjoy coloring the illustrations and reading these specially adapted Bible stories and will be inspired to go on to further reading of the Bible and other books of faith as well.

Adam and Eve in the Garden of Eden

After God created heaven and earth, and all the fish of the sea, and the birds of the air, and all the animals that lived on land, he decided to create human beings to watch and rule over them. He took the dust of the earth and from it created the first man, Adam. God took Adam and placed him in the warm and beautiful Garden of Eden, where there were plants and trees of all kinds, including many that produced fruit to eat. But Adam was lonely, for he had no one of his own kind to be his companion. God saw this, and so he created the first woman, Eve, as Adam's friend and helpmate, to share in all that God had created. Innocent and without care, Adam and Eve lived in Eden, not even needing clothes, and feeling no shame in not having any.

Now God told Adam and Eve that they could eat of the fruit of any tree in the Garden of Eden except one, the tree of the knowledge of good and evil. "The day you eat the fruit of this tree," God warned them, "you shall die."

Adam and Eve and all the other creatures lived peacefully together. But one creature, the sly serpent, was not content. Jealous of how happy the man and the woman were, he decided to do them harm. Entwining himself around the tree of the knowledge of good and evil, he waited for Eve to pass by, and upon seeing her alone called her over. "The fruit of this tree is very sweet," he told her. "Why not have some?"

"God has told us we may eat of the fruit of any tree except this one," she answered.

"If you eat this fruit, you shall become as powerful as God himself, which is why he has forbidden it to you," said the serpent.

The serpent continued to tempt Eve, and he was so persuasive that she could not resist him. She took fruit from the tree and began to eat it. Soon Adam joined her and he too found the fruit too tempting to resist. The serpent watched spitefully as they ate the fruit. When they had finished, all things suddenly seemed different. Now they felt ashamed of being naked and hurried to cover themselves with leaves. They were no longer innocent and happy and they knew what they had done would indeed anger God.

Genesis 3: 1–6

. . . she took the fruit of the tree thereof, and did eat,
and gave also unto her husband with her; and he did eat.

Adam and Eve driven out of the Garden of Eden

After Adam and Eve ate of the fruit of the tree of the knowledge of good and evil, they began to understand what God had not meant for them to know. They knew good and evil, and they knew fear. They understood for the first time that they were naked, and that they had done wrong. They sewed fig leaves together to cover themselves.

When they heard God walking in the garden in the cool of the day, they hid from Him. God called Adam to him, and Adam confessed that they had hidden because they were afraid, and because they were naked. From this, God understood that Adam and Eve had eaten the fruit of the tree, though he had forbidden them. God was angry.

Adam and Eve told God that the serpent had made them do it.

At this, God punished the serpent. He made the serpent the lowliest of beasts, compelled forever to slither on its belly on the ground.

And then God punished Adam and Eve. For wanting to be like gods and know what only God was meant to know, and so that Adam and Eve might not be tempted to eat of the fruit of the tree of life and become immortal, He drove them out of the Garden of Eden, expelling them into ordinary life. He created disharmony between man and woman; he created pain and sorrow; he made people forever after have to work for their food, and to grow old and die. "For dust thou art," said God, "and unto dust shalt thou return."

Because God still loved them, He showed them how to get their living from the soil and enjoy the fruits of their labor. He made for them clothing of animal skins. But outside the garden He placed angels with a flaming sword to make sure they never found their way back in.

Genesis 3: 23–24

Therefore the Lord God sent him forth from the garden of Eden,
to till the ground from whence he was taken.

Cain murders Abel

Eve bore Adam two sons. Cain, the elder, became a farmer, working in the fields. Abel, the younger, became a shepherd, caring for flocks of sheep.

Adam and Eve would thank God for their food and other blessings of life by making sacrificial offerings to Him. They would light a fire on an altar and burn offerings of grain, fruit, and animals they had killed. These were always the best of their kind, to show the proper gratitude to God.

When they became young men, Cain and Abel also made sacrifices. One day Abel freely sacrificed his finest young lambs, and God was pleased. That same day, Cain made an offering of grains and fruits from his harvest, but he didn't really want to sacrifice them, and God was not pleased. He didn't accept Cain's offering, and this made Cain angry.

God told Cain, "If you sacrifice freely, you do well, and I am pleased. If you begrudge me, I am not pleased. Why should you be angry?"

Cain became even angrier. He was jealous of Abel because God had accepted Abel's offering but not his. One day in the fields, Cain attacked his brother and killed him.

God asked Cain, "Where is your brother?" Cain replied, " I don't know. Am I my brother's keeper?" God knew the truth. He said, " What have you done? Your brother's voice cries out to me from the earth." And God cursed Cain.

God told him, "From now on you will never be able to make food grow from the earth. You will be a homeless fugitive and vagabond the rest of your life."

Cain was afraid and pleaded with God. "My punishment is too great to bear," he said. "If you drive me away I will be homeless. I will never see you again, and anyone who sees me may kill me."

But God made a mark upon Cain so that everyone would recognize him, and no one would harm him. God made sure that Cain suffered His punishment, and that no one would interfere.

Then Cain left the presence of God to dwell in a land east of Eden.

Genesis 4: 8–9

. . . when they were in the field, . . . Cain rose up against Abel his brother,
and slew him. . . . And the Lord said unto Cain, Where is Abel thy brother?
And he said, I know not: Am I my brother's keeper?

9

Noah and the animals entering the ark

The first people who populated the earth lived for hundreds of years. When a man named Noah was 600 years old, God became both sad and angry because most of the people he had created were doing terrible things—cheating, hurting, and killing each other. So God regretted that he had created human beings. He decided to destroy all of them, and with them all of the animals that lived on the earth.

God knew that Noah was a just man, though, so he chose to save him, his wife, their three sons, Shem, Ham, and Japheth, and the sons' wives. He warned Noah that soon a huge flood would cover the earth and kill every living creature that breathed air.

God told Noah exactly what to do to save his family. They should build an ark of gopher wood, sealed with pitch so it wouldn't leak. The ark had to be very large: 450 feet long, 75 feet wide, and 45 feet high. It was to have three levels, with many rooms and compartments built inside. It should have one window and one door.

Noah was told by God to collect at least two of each kind of animal, male and female, and take them into the ark. This included birds and reptiles, as well as four-footed animals of all sizes. Noah also had to load the ark with large supplies of every kind of food eaten by people and by animals.

Noah did everything as God ordered. When all had entered the ark, it began to rain very hard. The deluge continued for 40 days and 40 nights. The floodwaters rose until they were more than 20 feet deep, all over the earth. Even the highest mountains were covered. When the flood finally began to recede, the ark came down on the mountains of Ararat. Months later, Noah sent a raven from the ark's window, to see if the low ground was dry, but the raven flew far without finding a place to perch.

Noah tried again, this time with a dove, but it returned, unable to find anywhere to rest. A week later, Noah released the dove again. This time it brought back an olive leaf.

Soon they could leave the ark. After a full year on board, Noah's family went outside. God said that the people and the animals should multiply. He created the rainbow as a reminder to never again send a huge flood to destroy so many living creatures.

Genesis 7: 8–9

Every beast, all the cattle, every creeping thing, every fowl, every bird went to Noah and into the ark, two by two, as God had commanded him; and the Lord shut them in.

The Tower of Babel

After the flood sent by God drowned most living creatures many years passed, but still few people inhabited the earth. Noah and his wife were the ancestors of all. The people lived near the place where Noah's Ark had been when the long rain ended. Because everyone was together, all of the children learned a single language.

After moving west, these people settled on a plain they called Shinar, raising goats and sheep and growing wheat, flax, figs, grapes, and vegetables. This provided all they needed for food, clothing, houses, tools, and utensils. Work took a lot of time, but there also was music, dancing, and worship. To show gratitude for what the earth produced, they offered some of the best animals, fruits, and grains to God.

But as time passed, the people became dissatisfied. They became ambitious and puffed up with pride. They talked of doing some great thing, something never done before. They decided to build a large city, and a tower that would reach heaven. Soon people were digging, weaving baskets and sacks, cutting wood, or baking bricks. As the buildings went up, the tower stood above all.

Upon seeing this, God was displeased. He had created people who now wanted to leave the earth and join Him in heaven. They did not seek His approval. Soon they might totally forget their duty to honor and obey Him. So, when the city was large and the tower very high, God made the earth shake. Without any warning, the great tower cracked and quickly collapsed. Big chunks fell to the ground, scattering everyone below.

As the people screamed and shouted, something even worse happened. No one could understand most other people's words. God had made them speak many different languages. Unable to communicate, people began to distrust each other and to blame the others for the tower's downfall. Before long, each group left the ruined city to seek other places to live. The tower destroyed by God was afterward called the Tower of Babel.

Genesis 11: 5–9

The Lord confounded the people's language and scattered the people across the face of the earth. They did not try to rebuild the city or the tower.

Abraham and Isaac

Not far from where the Tower of Babel had once stood lived a wise and wealthy man named Abraham. Abraham was a good and pious man and God had special plans for him. He told him to leave his home and travel to a distant land. Abraham obeyed God and took his family and settled in a land called Canaan, where he lived happily and prospered.

One day, God decided to test Abraham's faith. He told Abraham to take his beloved only son, Isaac, and go to a mountain in the land of Moriah, and to sacrifice Isaac there as a burnt offering.

Abraham did as God told him. He gathered wood for a fire, and with Isaac and two servants, traveled for three days to the mountain. Leaving his servants at the foot of the mountain, carrying wood, fire, and knife, he and Isaac climbed upward.

Abraham had not told Isaac what God had commanded him to do. Isaac said to him, "Father, we have the fire and the wood, but where is the lamb for the sacrifice?" And Abraham replied, "God will provide a lamb."

When they reached the spot God had appointed, Abraham built an altar of stones. He placed the wood and prepared the fire. Then he bound the obedient Isaac and laid him upon the altar.

Abraham took the knife and prepared to sacrifice his beloved son. As he stretched out his hand, an angel of God called to him, saying: "Do not harm the boy, Abraham. For I know now that you love God so much that you were prepared to sacrifice your only son at his command."

Just then, Abraham saw a ram caught in a thicket. He took the ram and sacrificed it in place of Isaac.

And the angel said to Abraham, " Because you love God so truly, God will bless you. Your descendants will be numerous and powerful, because you have obeyed God and not withheld even your beloved son."

Genesis 22: 11–12

And he said, Lay not thine hand upon the lad, neither do thou any thing unto him:
for now I know that thou fearest God, seeing thou hast not withheld thy son . . .

Lot fleeing the destruction of Sodom and Gomorrah

Lot was the nephew of Abraham and had settled in the land of Canaan with him. After a while, he decided to move with his wife and daughters to a city in the valley. But Lot, who was a good man, did not know that this city, Sodom, and a city nearby, Gomorrah, were filled with evil people whose actions had outraged God. God decided to destroy the cities and the wicked people who lived there.

Lot was sitting at the city gate one evening when two angels of God, in the form of men, arrived there. He bowed and invited them to stay in his house that night. At his home, his family treated them well. After supper, though, a crowd of men surrounded the house. They had heard of the strangers and wanted to abuse them.

But Lot refused to hand the strangers over to them. Angered, they tried to break down the door to get at Lot and his family, but the angels blinded them, and sent them running in all directions.

The angels told Lot to gather his family and flee, because God had sent them to destroy the city. Lot's sons-in-law did not believe them. Their wives stayed with them. The angels escorted Lot, his wife, and his two unmarried daughters outside the city gate. They warned them not to look back and to hurry across the plain to the mountains for safety. Lot, afraid that they could not reach the distant mountains in time, begged God to spare the small city of Zoar on the plain, as a refuge. God granted this, then destroyed Sodom and Gomorrah at sunrise in a torrent of fire. Lot's wife couldn't resist looking behind them, and God turned her into a pillar of salt. After that Lot took his two daughters to live in a cave in the mountains.

Genesis 19: 24–26

Then the Lord rained on Sodom and Gomorrah brimstone and fire . . .
and he demolished those cities, and all on the plain . . .

Isaac is tricked into blessing Jacob

When Isaac, the son of Abraham, was grown he married a woman named Rebekah. They had two sons, Jacob and Esau, and lived in peace a long time and prospered.

One day when Isaac was old and had lost his sight, he called his elder son Esau, his favorite. Isaac told Esau to bring him a meal prepared in the way he liked best. "I am near death," he said. "Make me savory meat such as I love, so that I may eat and bless you before I die." Esau, a hunter, went to hunt for venison for his father.

Isaac's wife Rebekah overheard this. She called her younger son Jacob, who tended Isaac's flocks and was her favorite. "Bring me two young goats," she told him, "and I will make the meal for your father. You will bring it to him and he will bless you instead of Esau."

"But my brother is hairy, and I am smooth," Jacob replied. "My father will know that I am deceiving him and will not bless me but curse me." But Rebekah insisted. "The curse will be on me," she said. " Just do as I say."

Jacob killed the goats and brought Rebekah the skins and the meat. Rebekah cooked the meat the way Isaac liked. She then dressed Jacob in Esau's clothes, and covered his arms and neck with the woolly skins. Jacob then took the meal to Isaac.

"Who are you?" asked the blind Isaac.

"I am Esau, your elder son," said Jacob. "Here is the meal you asked me to bring; please give me your blessing." Isaac felt his hairy arms, but heard Jacob's voice, and was confused. But the hunter Esau's clothes smelled of the thickets, and Isaac was persuaded that Jacob was Esau. He ate. And he blessed Jacob before God, saying, "You will be my heir. You will prosper; you will rule the people; and you will rule over your brother."

Soon after Jacob left his father, Esau returned from his hunt. He too had made the savory meat Isaac loved, and now presented it to him, saying "Here is the meal you asked me to bring; please give me your blessing." And Isaac asked him, "Who are you?"

"I am Esau, your elder son," said Esau.

And then Isaac and Esau understood that Jacob had tricked them. Esau asked, "Have you no blessing for me?"

Isaac answered, "Before God I have made Jacob my heir and your master. What can I do for you?" And Esau wept bitterly.

Isaac told Esau that he would prosper, but that he would live by the sword and serve his brother. Esau felt hatred for his brother, and swore in his heart that after Isaac died, he would kill him.

Genesis 27: 22

And Jacob went near unto Isaac his father; and he felt him, and said,
The voice is Jacob's voice, but the hands are the hands of Esau.

Jacob's dream of the heavenly ladder

Rebekah saw the hatred that Esau felt for Jacob after he had cheated him of his father's blessing, so she decided to send Jacob away. She told Isaac that she did not want Jacob to take a wife from the Canaanites, among whom they lived, but rather from the family of her brother Laban. Isaac agreed that Jacob should go to him. So Jacob set out on his journey.

One night, he stopped at a certain place. He arranged some stones for his pillow, and lay down to sleep. And he had a dream.

In his dream, Jacob saw a ladder set upon the ground. The top of it reached to heaven, and Jacob saw angels of God going up and down.

At the very top stood God Himself. And God said to Jacob, " I am the God of Abraham and Isaac. This land upon which you lie, I give to you and to your descendants, who will be as numerous and widespread as the dust. I will be with you always, wherever you go, and I will bring you back to this land and will not leave you."

When Jacob awoke, he said to himself, "Surely God is in this place! This must be the gate of heaven." He arose, took the stones he had used for a pillow, and built a pillar with them. On the pillar he poured oil, and he made a vow to God: "If you will be with me, and protect me, and feed me, and clothe me, and let me return to my father's house in peace, then I will be devoted to you, and I will give a tenth of all I have to you."

Jacob declared that this pillar was God's house, and he named the place Bethel.

Genesis 28: 12

And he dreamed, and behold a ladder set up on the earth, and the top of it reached
to heaven: and behold the angels of God ascending and descending on it.

Jacob wrestling with the angel

As Jacob came near to Canaan, he sent messengers ahead to his brother Esau. He instructed them to tell Esau that Jacob was returning, with his family, servants, herds, and flocks, and wished to live in peace with his brother.

Soon the messengers returned and told Jacob that Esau was coming to meet him with 400 men.

Jacob was afraid. He divided his people and animals into two groups, so that if Esau attacked one, the other might escape and survive. Jacob then prayed to God to deliver him from the hand of Esau, reminding him of the requests for protection and favor he had made at Bethel.

The next day Jacob took goats, sheep, camels, cows, donkeys, and horses and had his servants deliver them to Esau as a gift, hoping to appease his brother's anger. He sent his two wives, his eleven sons, and two women servants to the far side of a river for safety. And then, alone, he waited to see what would happen.

That night as Jacob kept watch, someone came upon him from behind and began to wrestle with him. Neither could subdue the other, and they continued to wrestle the entire night.

At daybreak the stranger said, " Let me go." But Jacob would not, unless the stranger blessed him. The stranger asked, "What is your name?" When Jacob told him, he said, "You will no longer be called Jacob, but Israel, for you have fought with God and man, and have prevailed." Jacob asked, "What is your name?" and the stranger told him, "Do not ask my name." And the stranger blessed Jacob and left.

Then Jacob knew that he had been wrestling with God, and gave thanks that he had lived.

Genesis 32: 24–30

And he said, Thy name shall be called no more Jacob, but Israel: for as a prince hast thou power with God and with men, and hast prevailed.

Joseph sold into slavery by his brothers

Jacob had 12 sons and many daughters, born to his two wives, Leah and Rachel, and to two servants. When the youngest son, Benjamin, was a boy and Joseph was 17, Jacob gave Joseph a beautiful robe dyed with many colors from plants. He had a special love for Joseph, who was born when Jacob was very old. The ten older brothers knew this and were jealous. Also, after Joseph went to the distant pastures where they took their father's flocks, he told Jacob that they behaved badly. This made them more angry.

Their anger turned to hatred when Joseph told them of two dreams he had. In the first dream, the sheaves of wheat gathered by his brothers bowed down to his sheaf, which stood tall in the field. The second dream was more dramatic: in it, the sun, the moon, and 11 stars bowed down to Joseph. Even Jacob was angry at this. He thought Joseph meant that his father, his mother, and his 11 brothers would bow to him.

The next time Jacob sent Joseph to check on his brothers, they saw him when he still was far away and decided to kill him then and there. They agreed to throw his body into a pit and then tell their father that a wild animal must have eaten him. Reuben, Jacob's firstborn son, tried to save Joseph's life. He told the others not to shed blood. Instead, he said, throw Joseph into the pit unharmed and leave him there to die. Reuben planned to return later, rescue Joseph, and deliver him safely to his father. It was a good idea.

After Reuben left the camp, the other brothers saw a caravan of merchants passing at a distance. Judah saw a way to get rid of Joseph without killing him, and get money for him, too. So they hauled Joseph out of the pit and sold him to the strangers as a slave for 20 silver coins. When Reuben returned, the pit was empty. He was horrified. What could he tell their father now? The other brothers had poured a goat's blood on Joseph's special coat. When they took the flocks home, they showed the ruined coat to Jacob and said that they had found it on their way. This made the old man think that an animal had killed and eaten his son. Jacob's grief was great. No one could comfort him. Meanwhile, far away in Egypt, the merchants sold Joseph to the captain of the ruler's guard.

Genesis 37: 28

. . . and they drew and lifted Joseph out of the pit, and sold Joseph . . .
for twenty pieces of silver . . .

Joseph reveals himself to his brothers

In far-off Egypt, Joseph, through his wisdom and virtue, impressed Pharaoh, the ruler, so greatly that far from being a slave, he was made Pharaoh's chief minister. Time passed and Joseph prospered.

Now a time came when famine swept the land and everywhere people suffered. But in Egypt, through Joseph's wise management, food had been stored up, and there was plenty for all. In Canaan, Joseph's father sent his sons to Egypt to buy food. They were brought before Joseph, who was in charge of all such matters. Joseph knew immediately who they were, but the brothers, seeing Joseph in his splendid clothes, did not recognize him. Joseph was determined to punish them for what they had done to him. He pretended to think that they were spies and would let them take the grain only if they left one brother behind as a hostage and agreed to return to Egypt with their youngest brother, Benjamin, who had remained home.

The brothers agreed and returned to Canaan. But Jacob, fearing for the safety of Benjamin, would not allow him to go to Egypt, as Joseph had commanded. The grain ran out and the famine continued, however, and eventually Jacob told his sons to return to Egypt to buy more and to take Benjamin with them.

When the brothers arrived in Egypt, Joseph invited them to a great feast. Seeing Benjamin, Joseph asked, "Is this your youngest brother, of whom you spoke?" And Joseph had to leave the room, because he had begun to weep. Joseph could no longer restrain himself. He sent all his men, his servants, and the translator away and returned alone to his brothers.

"Don't you recognize me?" he asked, in their own language. "I am your brother Joseph, whom you sold into Egypt." The brothers were speechless and afraid.

"Do not be grieved or angry with yourselves," he said. "For it was not you who sent me here, but God. God has made me powerful in Egypt and has caused me to save your lives." And Joseph embraced his brother Benjamin and wept; he embraced all his brothers and wept.

After this, Joseph asked his brothers to bring their father, Jacob, to Egypt. When Pharaoh learned of this, he invited all of Jacob's family to come to Egypt.

Genesis 45: 1–4

And he said, I am Joseph your brother, whom ye sold into Egypt.

Finding of Moses

When Joseph had been with Pharaoh for a long time, Jacob and his entire family joined him. God had told Jacob that he would be called Israel, so Jacob's big family was known as "the children of Israel." Soon Jacob died, and in time so did his sons, but each man and his wife left children, who in turn had children. The families of Jacob's 12 sons, later called "the 12 tribes of Israel," grew to be so big that the Egyptians became nervous. After Pharaoh who favored Joseph died, the new pharaoh said that "the children of Israel"—foreigners with their own religion—might help Egypt's enemies.

So Pharaoh made the men of Israel do hard labor as slaves, under strict supervisors, and their families lived in poverty and fear. Then Pharaoh decided to be even more harsh. He ordered the two midwives who helped the women of Israel in childbirth to kill every male child that was born. After the men of Israel all died, he thought, the young women would marry Egyptian men and have Egyptian children.

The two women bravely ignored Pharaoh's cruel order. They claimed that the women of Israel gave birth so quickly that often the baby was safely tucked away before they arrived! Now the angry ruler told the Egyptian people to throw into the river every male child born to the people of Israel. This caused great grief among the families.

However, one woman managed to hide her baby son for three months. She could not hide him forever, though, so one day she wove a basket of reeds that could float. She put the handsome baby in it near the river, hoping that an Egyptian woman would find and adopt him. Her young daughter, Miriam, hid nearby and watched. She was afraid when a daughter of Pharaoh, with her servants, came to the spot to bathe. When the basket was opened, the Egyptian princess knew this must be a child of Israel whose mother was trying to save his life. She did not seem to want to kill the baby, so Miriam got up all her courage and offered to bring a woman of Israel to provide mother's milk for the child. Of course, she fetched the baby's own mother! Pharaoh's daughter paid her to nourish the child. When he was a little older she took him as her son and named him Moses.

Exodus 2: 6

And the daughter of Pharaoh came down to wash herself
at the river . . . .she saw the child . . . she had compassion on him,
and said, This is one of the Hebrews' children.

29

Moses and Aaron before Pharaoh

Moses was raised as a prince of Egypt and grew to manhood. But he was troubled by the harsh treatment of the Israelites by the Egyptians, and one day, struck an Egyptian overseer and killed him. To escape punishment, he fled and settled in the land of Midian, where he married and lived peacefully. But God had a special plan for Moses.

One day on the mountain called Horeb, God appeared in the form of a burning bush and spoke to Moses. He told Moses to go before Pharaoh and tell him, in the name of God, to let the people of Israel go, that they may serve their God. Moses returned to Egypt and did as God had commanded him, but Pharaoh would not listen.

Instead Pharaoh ordered that the Hebrews' labor be made more difficult. "They must make as many bricks as ever, but must find their own materials. Make them do more work," said Pharaoh, "and they will not concern themselves with serving their God."

When the people were unable to do all the work they had been ordered to do, Pharaoh's taskmasters beat their foremen and made their lives even more miserable.

So Moses asked God, "Why have you not delivered us? Since I spoke to Pharaoh in your name, he has only done us more harm." And God replied, "You shall see what I will make Pharaoh do. I have heard the groaning of your people, and I have not forgotten the covenant I made with Abraham. Pharaoh shall drive you from Egypt, and I shall deliver you into the land I promised your fathers."

God told Moses and his brother Aaron to tell Pharaoh again to let the Israelites go.

"When you speak to Pharaoh again," God told them, "he will demand a miracle. And Aaron will cast down his rod, and it shall become a serpent."

Moses and Aaron did as God commanded, and went before Pharaoh again. And Aaron did cast down his rod, and it became a serpent.

Pharaoh then called for his wise men and sorcerers. And they cast down their rods also, and they became serpents. But Aaron's rod swallowed up their rods.

But God had hardened Pharaoh's heart, and again he refused to let the Israelites go.

Exodus 7: 10

. . . and Aaron cast down his rod before Pharaoh, and before his servants,
and it became a serpent.

Moses parts the Red Sea

Pharaoh was told that the people of Israel had fled. He said, "Why have we let the Israelites go? Why should they not continue to serve us?" And he gathered his horsemen, and his chariots, and his army, and pursued the Israelites to their encampment by the sea.

When Pharaoh's army came near, the Israelites were afraid. To Moses they cried, "Have you brought us to die in the wilderness? Wouldn't it have been better to stay and serve the Egyptians, than to come here and die?"

Moses told them, " Fear not, God will save us, and we will never see the Egyptians again. Do not question God."

Now God told Moses to bring the people to the sea. "Stretch out your hand over the water," he commanded, "and the water will divide, and the people may walk through the sea on dry land. The Egyptians will follow you, and then I will cause them to know that I am God."

Moses did as he was told. God caused a strong wind to blow all night, and divided the water. The Israelites walked through the water on dry land, with a wall of water on their left, and a wall of water on their right. And Pharaoh's army followed them.

In the morning, when all the Egyptians were in the sea, God caused the wheels to come off their chariots. And he told Moses, stretch out your hand over the sea, and the waters will come together again. Moses did so. The Egyptians attempted to flee, but the water covered them, and their horses and chariots, and not one escaped. The Israelites continued on dry land until they reached the other shore of the sea, and were saved.

When the people saw what God had done, they believed in God, and obeyed His servant Moses.

Exodus 14: 27–28

And the waters returned, and covered the chariots, and the horsemen,
and all the host of Pharaoh . . .

Moses comes down from Mt. Sinai with the tablets of the law

After the Israelites had escaped the Egyptians, God called Moses to him again on the mountain, so that he might give him the laws and commandments that he wished the people of Israel to follow. Moses was on the mountain with God for 40 days and 40 nights.

The people grew weary of waiting for Moses. They came to Aaron and said, "Make us a god, so we may worship it. We no longer care what happens to Moses." Aaron, unsure what to do, collected their gold jewelry and melted it down. He then made of it a figure of a calf and placed it on an altar, saying, "This is the God that brought you out of Egypt." He declared a special feast day, and the people made offerings and celebrated.

When God saw this, he told Moses to return to the people right away. "They have turned aside from my commandments," He said. "They are a stubborn and willful people. I am going to destroy them."

Moses pleaded with God not to destroy the Israelites. He reminded God of the promises he had made to Abraham, Isaac, and Jacob, that their descendants would live in Canaan and be numerous and great. And God relented.

God had given Moses stone tablets on which he had written his laws and commandments, and Moses carried them down the mountain to the Israelites' camp. But when he saw the golden calf, and the people celebrating, he was so angry that he threw the tablets to the ground and broke them. Moses called to the people, saying, "Whoever is on God's side, stand with me." To those who joined him, he said, "God has commanded that those who worship the calf must die. Take your swords and kill them, even if they are your brothers, your friends, or your neighbors."

Three thousand people were killed that day. The next day, Moses announced that he would ask God to forgive the people for their sin. When he did, God told him: "Whoever has sinned against me, I will blot out of my book. I will keep my promises to Abraham, Isaac, and Jacob, but I will punish the people first."

And then God sent a plague on the people of Israel.

Exodus 32: 15–16

And Moses turned, and went down from the mount,
and the two tables of the testimony were in his hand . . . and the writing
was the writing of God, graven upon the tables.

35

Battle of Jericho

During the 40 years of wandering in the desert, the men and women who had left Egypt with Moses all had died. They never saw Canaan, the land God had promised their people. This happened because they had not obeyed God. Many children had been born, though. When they became men and women they had children of their own, so the 12 tribes of Israel had more people than ever. They had to cross the wide, deep river Jordan to reach the city of Jericho, which they had to capture so they could possess the land of Canaan. After everyone crossed the river and ate some grain, their leader, Joshua, met a man with a sword, who said he was the captain of God's army (an angel).

The gates in the high stone wall around Jericho were closed. The men inside were ready to defend their homes from the 40,000 men of Israel who would attack. God told Joshua what should be done. For six days in a row, soon after dawn, every fighting man got in line and marched around the city wall. Behind them, seven priests walked in front of the ark of the Covenant. Each priest had a ram's horn (called a shofar), which was used in battle as trumpets and bugles were used later. The women, children, and old men followed. The thousands of people uttered no word or sound as they walked, but the priests blew the horns. Each morning the men on the walls of Jericho watched and the people in their houses listened as this eerie procession circled the city. They waited fearfully for the attack.

On the seventh day, as God had instructed, the people of Israel marched around the city seven times, silently except for the sound of the horns. Suddenly the priests gave a long signal blast on the horns and the people all shouted as loudly as they could. At that moment, the protective wall around Jericho crumbled to the ground. The fighting men of Israel ran forward over the rubble. They killed every man, woman, and child in the city, and the animals, too. Only Rahab's family was saved. She had sheltered two spies sent to the city by Joshua in advance. All the items in the city made of gold, silver, bronze, or iron were taken for the worship of God. Then the buildings were burned to the ground.

Joshua 6: 20

When the people heard the sound of the trumpet, . . . and . . .
shouted with a great shout, . . . the wall fell down flat . . . . And they
utterly destroyed all that was in the city . . .

Gideon defeats the Midianites

Once again the Israelites had sinned by worshipping other gods, and to punish them God allowed the Midianites to rule over them for seven years. Their harvests were stolen and destroyed; they were at the mercy of their enemies, and they cried out to God.

One day a stranger appeared before a young Israelite named Gideon, the youngest son of a farmer.

"God is with you," said the stranger, "you are a mighty man of valor, and you shall save the Israelites."

"If God is with us," said Gideon, "why are we suffering so? God has abandoned us. As for me, I am the youngest son of a poor family. What can I do?"

And the stranger said, "I shall be with you, and you shall defeat the Midianites." Gideon feared the stranger, and asked for a sign. The stranger asked that food be brought to him. Gideon brought it and he set it on a rock. At the stranger's touch the rock burst into flame and consumed the food, and the stranger disappeared. Gideon knew that he was an angel of God.

That night, God told Gideon to destroy the altar of the god Baal that had been set up by his father, Joash, and to replace it with an altar to God. Gideon did so. When the men of the city saw what he had done, they determined to kill him. They went to Joash and demanded that he surrender Gideon to them. But Joash said, "Why does Baal need you to defend him? If he really is a god, let him punish Gideon himself." And of course nothing happened.

The Midianites gathered a huge army to destroy the Israelites. Gideon asked for a sign that God would save them through him, and God gave one. Gideon gathered an army of Israelites and followed the Midianites to their camp.

God saw this, and said to Gideon, "You have too many people with you. If you defeat the Midianites, they will think they did it themselves without my help." So Gideon sent 22,000 of them away, keeping 10,000 with him.

And God saw this, and said, "You still have too many. Bring them to the river to drink. Keep everyone who laps up the water like a dog, and send the rest away." After this only 300 men were left to fight the enormous Midianite host.

That night God told Gideon to attack. Gideon sneaked into the Midianite camp to hear what the men were saying. One man had had a dream that was interpreted as a prophecy of the sword of Gideon destroying the Midianite host, and the men were afraid. Gideon felt strong, and told his men to have confidence.

Gideon gave his 300 men trumpets and pitchers with burning lamps inside, and led them to the Midianite camp. At his signal, they all broke the pitchers; holding up the lamps in one hand and their swords in the other, they shouted, "The sword of the Lord and of Gideon!"

The Midianites panicked and ran about in confusion. Gideon's men blew the trumpets, and God set the Midianites against each other. Those who were not killed fled, and the army of the Israelites pursued them out of the country.

Judges 7: 19–23

And the three hundred blew the trumpets, and the Lord set every man's sword against his fellow, even throughout all the host . . .

Delilah cutting the hair of Samson

When the Philistines had ruled the people of Israel for 40 years, an angel told Manoah's wife, who never had gotten pregnant, that she would have a son, who would begin to free the Israelites. The boy was named Samson at his birth. When he was a young man he married a Philistine woman. His father and mother did not understand why, but it was part of God's plan. Soon, in a series of vengeful conflicts with the Philistine men, Samson outdid his opponents. Finally, the Philistines invaded the land of Israel. They wanted to capture and kill Samson, who was alone on a mountaintop.

The men of Israel, not knowing why Samson had provoked this trouble, went to him and said they would hand him over to the Philistines. Samson did not protest, after they promised not to kill him themselves. At the Philistines' camp, Samson broke the strong ropes that bound his hands, as if they were weak threads. Then he grabbed the heavy, sun-bleached jawbone of a donkey from the ground and used it to beat to death a thousand Philistines. He believed that God enabled him to do this. Then, tired and thirsty, he called upon God to give him water, and it flowed from a hole in the jawbone.

Samson continued to use his amazing strength to defeat the Philistines. Then their leaders secretly offered a huge amount of money to a woman, Delilah, to find out what made him so strong. Delilah tried three times to learn Samson's secret, but each time he tricked her. She awakened him from sleep to "warn" him that enemies were near, after she thought she had taken away his strength. He never weakened. The third time, he walked off with a heavy beam tied to his hair, as if it were a toothpick.

One day Samson gave in to Delilah's entreaties. He told her that, with his head shaved, he would be no stronger than an average man. Later, while he slept with his head on her lap, a man shaved his hair. When Delilah "warned" him that enemies were near, Samson expected no trouble, as usual. He had lost the special power God had given him, though, by telling Delilah the secret. He was unprotected. The Philistines captured him, gouged out his eyes, and put him in prison.

Judges 16: 18–19

And when Delilah . . . made him sleep upon her knees
and she called for a man, and she caused him to shave off the seven locks
of his head; . . . and his strength went from him.

Samson destroying the temple

The Philistines were gleeful. They finally had overcome Samson when the seductive Delilah discovered the secret of his supernatural strength. Their leaders gladly gave her the promised money, as soon as he had been taken prisoner. Meanwhile, Samson was in terrible pain, alone in the prison cell with no hope of help or rescue. He cursed himself for giving in to Delilah's treacherous pleas. For several weeks the Philistines left Samson in prison. They were pleased that he was suffering and powerless, and they no longer had to fear the power his God had given him.

After a while, the Philistine leaders decided to make a spectacle of Samson. Everyone whose family members and friends had been killed by him would enjoy his downfall. The people would gloat, tormenting Samson who had terrorized their men.

A youth led Samson from the prison. A multitude was assembled in the temple to see him be poked, prodded, hit, and tripped, without being able to see who did it. Samson now had no more strength than any other man of his size, so he only had ropes binding his arms. He could not see to run away, so his legs were left free. As he neared the overhanging porch of the temple, many people jostled to peer at him from the interior of the building and from the flat roof. They jeered as he approached.

No one realized that Samson's having had his head shorn for the first time had not made him lose his great strength forever. His hair had grown back while he was in prison. Samson had nothing more to lose and no hope of escape. He decided to kill as many Philistines as he could and end his own misery. He asked the youth at his elbow to stop near the pillars at the temple's main entrance. Then Samson braced himself between the two pillars and pulled as if he still had the enormous strength that had awed the Philistines. At first nothing happened, but as he strained every muscle the pillars cracked and tumbled. The temple came crashing down. Many people were crushed beneath the falling blocks of stone. Others were hurt or killed when they fell to the ground.

Judges 16: 30

And Samson said, Let me die with the Philistines. And he bowed himself with
all his might; and the house fell upon . . . all the people that were therein.

David and Goliath

When the Philistines invaded the land of the Israelites, they camped above a valley. The Israelites, led by Saul, faced them across the valley. Instead of preparing for battle, though, the Philistines sent one man forward. Goliath was 10 feet tall. His helmet and body armor were made of brass. His iron-pointed wooden spear seemed to be as big as a roof beam. With his gigantic shield and heavy sword, he strode toward the Israelites and bellowed a challenge. He shouted that if any Israelite fought him alone, and killed him, the Philistines would serve the Israelites from then on. If Goliath won the fight, though, the Israelites would have to serve the Philistines.

No Israelite felt able to defeat Goliath. If they accepted his terms and their man was killed, they all would become slaves. Anyway, would the Philistines really submit to them peacefully, even if one of them somehow killed Goliath? If they chose to fight army-to-army, could they defeat the Philistines, who had the fearsome Goliath? For 40 mornings in a row, Goliath shouted his challenge. The Israelites were silent, ashamed but afraid.

David, the youngest son of Jesse, tended his father's flocks. One day his father sent him to bring bread and cheese to his three oldest brothers, who were in the army, and to bring back news of them. Goliath shouted his daily challenge soon after David reached the army. The two armies would battle today, if no one agreed to fight Goliath alone.

David was enraged to hear this man defy the Israelite army, which to him was the army of God. The soldiers heard him say this and brought him to Saul. David declared that he would kill Goliath. When Saul said that he was too young and unused to war, David bragged that he had killed a lion and a bear that attacked his father's sheep. He refused the armor Saul wanted to lend him and set out with only his shepherd's stick, five stones in his pouch, and his sling. Running toward Goliath, he shot his first stone. It struck the giant's forehead and he fell like a tree. David quickly cut off Goliath's head with his own sword. Seeing this, the Philistines fled, instead of keeping their promise to serve the Israelites. Many of them were killed as the jubilant Israelites chased them a long way.

I Samuel 17: 49–51

Therefore David ran, and stood upon the Philistine, and took his sword, and drew it out of the sheath thereof, and . . cut off his head therewith.

Saul has the Witch of En-dor
summon the spirit of Samuel

David had fled to Gath and was serving the Philistine ruler there, and the Philistines were gathering their armies for battle against the Israelites. Saul, the king, saw the size of the Philistine forces and was afraid. The great leader Samuel had died, so Saul could not seek his help. He sought help from God, but God did not answer him.

So Saul instructed his servants to find one who could call up spirits. They found such a woman in En-dor, and one night Saul disguised himself and went to her. "Please," he said, " call up the spirit of the one I wish to speak to."

"You know," she replied, "that I must not, because Saul has forbidden such things. He has banished the wizards and seers and other such people from the land, under pain of death. Do you wish to entrap me? Do you want me to die?"

The woman spoke the truth, but Saul was desperate. He swore to her in the name of God that no harm would come to her.

"To whom do you wish to speak?" she asked.

"Bring me Samuel," said Saul. And Samuel appeared.

At this, the woman understood who Saul was, and was afraid. "Why have you deceived me?" she cried. But Saul assured her again that she would be safe.

"Why have you disturbed me?" Samuel demanded of Saul.

"I am distressed," answered Saul. "The Philistines make war against me, and God has left me. You must tell me what to do."

"Why ask me?" said Samuel. "God himself has left you and become your enemy. You have disobeyed him by allowing your enemy Amalek to live. God will give your kingdom to David. Tomorrow you and your sons will be killed in battle, and your armies will be destroyed by the Philistines."

On hearing this, Saul fell to the ground and was afraid.

I Samuel 28: 11

Then said the woman, Whom shall I bring up unto thee?
And he said, Bring me up Samuel.

Solomon and the baby

When Solomon, son of David, became king of Israel, God asked him in a dream what he wanted given to him. Solomon requested the ability to judge wisely and make good decisions. He knew that he needed help to rule well. God was pleased. The king could have asked to live longer than others, or to have immense riches. Instead, he wanted a gift that would help all of the people. So, God not only granted the wish, he said that Solomon would have great riches and honors, and a long, satisfying life. When Solomon awoke, he traveled to the great city of Jerusalem. There he made offerings to God, offered thanks for peace, and provided a feast. The kings of Israel were judges as well as rulers. They had to decide what to do when there was a conflict. Soon Solomon's great wisdom was tested.

Two women went to the king to judge their quarrel. One woman stated that both of them lived in one house, with no one else. She had given birth to a baby boy; three days later, the other woman had done the same. The first woman said that the other woman's child must have suffocated during the night, soon afterward, when his mother rolled over on him without realizing it. The next morning, the first woman awoke to find a dead baby next to her. Soon she realized that the dead child was not her son. Then she saw that her healthy baby was with the other woman. She told the king that the other woman must have realized during the night that she accidentally had killed her child. To make up for her loss and to hide her terrible mistake, she must have gotten up and switched the live child with it.

At this point the second woman shouted that the living baby was hers. The first woman insisted that she knew her own baby. No one could tell who was lying. The king was silent. Then he stopped the buzz of opinions by calling for a sword. When it was brought, Solomon ordered a soldier to cut the living child in half so each woman could have a part. As the people gasped at this awful "solution," the first woman pleaded, "Give the child to her, do not kill it." At the same time, the second woman said grimly, "So be it. Divide it." Then everyone knew that only the first woman loved the child. Solomon returned the baby to her, and she was greatly relieved and glad.

I Kings 3: 19–28

Then the king answered and said, Give her the living child . . .
she is the mother thereof.

Solomon and the Queen of Sheba

Solomon reigned as king and judge of Israel for 40 years. During that time many cities were built and improved. Most important of all, he personally planned a large, beautiful temple built on high ground in Jerusalem, for the worship of God. Solomon had God's promise that he and the people would prosper and receive mercy. However, He had warned that if they worshipped other gods, as their ancestors had, the temple, city, and kingdom would be ruined, and the people would suffer. The temple and a magnificent palace were completed when Solomon had reigned for 20 years. Before marrying a daughter of Egypt's Pharaoh (ruler), he had a separate palace built for her, because the ark of the Covenant, kept in the king's palace, had made it a holy place. Solomon ruled from the river Jordan to Egypt's border, and in Lebanon. Fragrant cedar trees from there shaded and beautified Jerusalem. The Hittites, Amorites, and all whose ancestors had lived in the land of Canaan before Joshua led the people of Israel there were taxed. No people of Israel were slaves, as their ancestors had been before fleeing from Egypt with Moses.

The Queen of Sheba, whose land was in Arabia, heard many stories about Solomon's wisdom and power, and about splendid Jerusalem. She decided to see for herself whether this ruler was as outstanding as merchants and diplomats had said he was. Many people worked long hours to prepare for her journey to the land of Israel with hundreds of officials, attendants, and servants.

The queen's servants loaded a caravan of camels with fragrant spices, ornaments and objects made of gold, and precious jewels not found in the land of Israel. When the queen was in Solomon's presence, she asked many questions and also observed what he did. Soon she was convinced that he was even wiser than she had heard. Also, she was very impressed by his palace, his officials' behavior, the people's clothing (even the servants'), the meals served, and Solomon's visits to the temple where the God of Israel was worshipped. The queen said that the people were fortunate to have him as king, and to be blessed by God. The two rulers gave each other valuable gifts before she left.

II Chronicles: 9

And when the queen of Sheba had seen the wisdom of Solomon, . . .
she said, . . . half of the greatness of thy wisdom was not told me:
for thou exceedest the fame that I heard.

Elijah taken to Heaven in a fiery chariot

Elijah was one of the great prophets of God, calling constantly for the people of Israel and Judah to turn from the Canaanite god Baal back to the God of their fathers. Elisha was Elijah's pupil and follower.

One day God made it known to Elijah that his days were ending, and that he would take him up into heaven in a whirlwind.

Elijah told Elisha to leave him, but Elisha would not. "As long as God lives, and as long as you live, I will not leave you," Elisha said. So they went to Beth-el, and then to Jericho.

At each place, prophets met them and asked Elisha, "Do you know that God will take Elijah from you today?"

"Yes, I know," answered Elisha. "Don't speak of it."

At each place, Elijah told Elisha to stay while he went on, and Elisha would not.

Finally Elijah and Elisha came to the bank of the Jordan river. Elijah took his cloak and folded it up. He struck the surface of the water with it, and the water divided, opening a path on which they walked to the other side.

When they had crossed the river, Elijah said, "Tell me what I can do for you before I am taken away." And Elisha said, "Give me a double portion of your spirit."

In those days, a double portion was the inheritance a father gave his eldest son.

Elijah replied, "You have asked something very hard. If God allows you to see me when I go, he will give you what you ask; if you can't see me, then he will not."

As they were talking, there appeared a chariot of fire, pulled by horses of fire. A whirlwind arose and pulled Elijah into the chariot, and the chariot ascended to heaven. Elijah was gone. Elisha saw this, and cried, "My father, my father! The chariot of Israel!" And he knew that God had chosen him as Elijah's successor.

Elisha tore his clothes to show that he was in mourning. He picked up Elijah's cloak and struck the water with it, and again a path opened to let him walk to the other side of the river, and he returned to Jericho.

When the prophets saw him, they exclaimed, "The spirit of Elijah is in him." And they bowed down before him.

II Kings 2: 11–12

. . . there appeared a chariot of fire, and parted them both asunder;
and Elijah went up by a whirlwind into heaven.

Sennacherib's army destroyed by the angel

When Hoshea was king of Israel, Hezekiah became king of Judah. He trusted in God and kept all his commandments. God was with him, and he prospered.

Hezekiah rebelled against Assyria, the great empire which ruled over all the smaller kingdoms at that time. He refused to serve the Assyrian king. The Assyrians came and conquered Samaria and Israel, taking the people into captivity. Then they attacked Judah, capturing all the cities except Jerusalem.

Hezekiah decided to surrender. He gave to Sennacherib, the Assyrian king, all the silver and gold from the temple and from the king's house.

But Sennacherib sent to Jerusalem a huge army, and a message to be delivered to the people by his commander Rab-shakeh. "Hear the word of the great king of Assyria," he cried. "Do not be deceived by Hezekiah, for he cannot save you. You and your king trust in your God, but so did the people of the other lands we have conquered. Their gods could not help them. Why do you think yours is any better?"

When Rab-shakeh's words were reported to Hezekiah, he sent his advisors to the prophet Isaiah. Isaiah told them not to be afraid. God would cause Sennacherib to leave to fight other enemies, and to be killed by the sword in his own country.

Sennacherib then heard that the Ethiopians had sent an army against him. He made plans to move against them. But first he sent word to Hezekiah that his army would capture Jerusalem, just as it had captured Samaria and Israel and so many other lands before.

Hezekiah prayed to God, saying, "It is true that Sennacherib has conquered many lands, and cast their gods into the fire. But they were false gods. Will you not save us, so that the world may know that you are the true and only God?"

God sent his answer through Isaiah, who told Hezekiah that God had told him:

"I have heard your prayer. To Sennacherib I say, Jerusalem laughs at you. You have blasphemed me, and reproached me, and threatened me. Don't you know who I am? Haven't you heard what I have done? Because you offend me, I will turn you away. Sennacherib's army will not come into Jerusalem. I will save it, for my own sake and for the sake of my servant David."

And so it came to pass that night, that an angel of God went into the camp of the Assyrians, numbering 185,000, and struck them dead.

Sennacherib returned to his capital, Nineveh. Soon he was assassinated by two of his own sons.

II Kings 19: 35–36

And it came to pass that night, that the angel of the Lord went out, and smote in the camp of the Assyrians an hundred four-score and five thousand: and when they arose early in the morning, behold, they were all dead corpses.

55

Job hearing of his ruin

Job was careful to obey all of God's commandments. He was honest, generous, and peaceful with other people, and he offered some of the best of the products of his land to God daily, by burning the animals, fruits, and grains on an altar. He even made special burnt offerings (called sacrifices) for each of his sons, in case one had offended God.

According to the writers of the Old Testament, one day God was talking with Satan (also called "the devil"). Satan, a former angel, had rebelled against God and had been banished from Heaven. He constantly tried to get people to disobey God. On this occasion, God bragged to Satan that Job always did the right thing. Satan replied that Job had no reason to behave badly, as God had blessed everything he did and had. He and his family lived happily and prosperously. Said Satan, "If you destroyed some of the good things he enjoys, or made him unhappy, then he would curse you." To prove that Satan was wrong, God told him to do anything he wanted to Job's property but not to harm him bodily. God was sure that Job would remain obedient, even if disaster struck him.

Satan didn't do things in a small way. Soon after that, when Job was at home, one of his servants rushed up shouting that Sabeans had attacked the workers on his farmland, killing all of them except him, and taking all of the oxen and donkeys. A moment later, another servant ran to Job, gasping, and said that fire from the sky had burned up all of Job's sheep and the shepherds, too, except him. Before Job could react, a third man pushed them aside to report that the Chaldeans had stolen all of his camels and merchandise, and slaughtered the servants taking them to market. Then a fourth man arrived with the worst news of all. He said that all of Job's sons and their wives had been enjoying a meal together at the oldest brother's house. (Job knew this was true.) Suddenly, the servant reported, a tremendously strong wind came up. The roof and walls of the house collapsed and crushed the young people and the servants. He alone escaped.

Job stood up and tore his clothing in grief. Then he fell to the ground—and worshipped God. He said, "God gave, and God has taken away; blessed be God."

Job 1: 15–21

Then Job arose, . . . and said, . . . the Lord gave,
and the Lord hath taken away; blessed be the name of the Lord.

Shadrach, Meshach, and Abed-nego in the fiery furnace

Nebuchadnezzar, king of an empire with many provinces, governed from the splendid city of Babylon. His famous hanging gardens astonished all who saw them, they were so beautiful and so skillfully designed. With his great power and wealth, all he did was grand. So, when Nebuchadnezzar set up an image for the people to worship, the statue was 90 feet tall, 9 feet wide—and covered with beaten gold. It stood on a plain outside the city. As soon as the statue was in place, the king ordered every official, from the highest to the lowest, in every province he ruled, to attend the dedication ceremony. On that day, a huge crowd of men gathered in front of the statue. The king's herald shouted, "People of all nations and languages, when you hear the sound of the horns, the flutes, the harps, and the other instruments, you must lie on the ground face-down and worship the golden image. Anyone who does not will be thrown alive into a fiery furnace."

When the music sounded, every man there seemed to worship the statue, as the king demanded. Not every man was there, though! Nebuchadnezzar had appointed three Jews to administer the province of Babylon. Some Chaldean men told the king that these Jews, named Shadrach, Meshach, and Abed-nego, refused to worship the golden image. Nebuchadnezzar was very angry to hear that he had been defied, but he gave the three men a chance to prove that the accusation was untrue, or to change their minds and do as he ordered. The three replied that, even if they were in a fiery furnace, their one God would save them from harm. Again they refused to worship the king's gods.

The king was enraged. Soldiers tied the men's hands and feet together. The fire was made extra hot. The high flames burned some of the soldiers to death as they neared the furnace, but others threw the three Jews in. Everyone was astonished when the men walked through the flames, unharmed. Nebuchadnezzar called to them to come out. They and their clothes had not been burnt at all. The king now realized that the God of Israel had power not shown by any other god. He decreed that people who did not respect the God of the Jews would be killed, and their homes destroyed.

Daniel 3: 24

Then Nebuchadnezzar the king . . . rose up in haste . . . and said to
his counselors, Did we not cast three men bound into the midst of the fire?

Daniel in the lions' den

Belshazzar, son of Nebuchadnezzar, did not learn from his father's experience. When he was king, he stole the golden goblets the Jews used to worship God, and used them at feasts. He worshipped images of many gods. One day, mysterious words appeared written on a palace wall. The people were frightened. Belshazzar demanded that Daniel, a Jewish official in Babylon, interpret the message. Daniel said that God was ending his rule. That night, Belshazzar was killed and Darius, the Median ruler, took the kingdom. Daniel was very capable and honest, so Darius made him one of his three highest officials, to supervise the king's business. Darius was so pleased with Daniel's work that he wanted to let him make all decisions for Babylon. The lower officials became very jealous of Daniel's success. Soon they thought of a way to have him killed.

These men told the king that, to encourage everyone to give him the greatest honor and respect, he should proclaim that, for thirty days, no one could make a request to any god or man except to him, Darius. Seeing nothing wrong with this idea, the king signed a decree saying that the punishment for anyone who disobeyed would be to be put into a den of hungry lions. The laws of his people said that a king's decree could not be changed.

Daniel prayed to God three times a day, openly. The jealous officials sprang their trap. The king, they said, must punish Daniel for disobeying his decree—which, they reminded him, could not be changed. The king was disgusted that he had been tricked, and tried all day to avoid having Daniel killed, but at sundown he sent him to the lions' den. He told Daniel sincerely that he hoped his God would save him. That night the king did not eat or listen to music, and could not sleep, he was so upset. Very early in the morning he went to the lions' den and called out, asking if Daniel's God had saved him. Daniel calmly replied that he was unharmed, because he had done no wrong. Darius gladly had Daniel released. The men who had planned his death were put in his place. Darius proclaimed that all should worship the God of the Jews, who had shown his power. Daniel was more highly favored than ever, even after Cyrus, the Persian, became king.

Daniel 6: 22

My God has sent his angel and has shut the lions' mouths, so that
they have not hurt me, because I was found innocent by him;
and neither have I done you any harm, O king.

Jonah being swallowed by the whale

God spoke to Jonah, telling him to go to the city of Nineveh and warn the people there that God was angry because of their bad behavior. Jonah did not want to go. So, he got on a ship sailing to Tarshish. He hoped to avoid God's command by going far away.

The sky was clear and the water was calm, but when the ship was far out at sea, suddenly a strong wind began blowing and a terrible rainstorm began. The waves battered the small wooden ship and washed over the deck. The sailors and passengers were afraid the ship would sink. They even threw valuable merchandise overboard to make the ship lighter, so it might float longer. Each man prayed to his gods to save his life. All this time, Jonah was sleeping, not even aware of the danger.

The captain found Jonah, shook him awake, and ordered him to pray to his own god. As the storm got worse, the desperate sailors decided that Jonah was to blame for the terrible danger they were in. He already had told them that he was fleeing to avoid obeying God's command. Now he said that if they threw him into the sea, they would be safe. The men, even more afraid now, tried hard to row the ship to shore, but the storm got even worse. Finally they did throw Jonah overboard. They hoped his god would be satisfied when he drowned, and would end the storm as quickly as it had started.

When Jonah hit the water, the sea became calm. Everyone on the ship was safe—but in a moment Jonah was swallowed by a whale! For three days he was in the huge creature's belly. He thanked God for saving him from drowning, and said he would obey God's words from now on. Then God caused the whale to spew Jonah out onto land. He told Jonah again to go to Nineveh and warn the people to stop their violent way of living.

This time Jonah traveled to the great city and began to preach. To his surprise, the people believed his message that God would destroy the place after 40 days because they were doing wrong. From the king to the poorest servants, they fasted and wore rough clothes to show that they were sorry. They hoped that God would give them another chance. When He saw the people trying to do better, He decided not to punish them.

Jonah 1: 15–17

So they took up Jonah, and cast him forth into the sea . . . .
Now the Lord had prepared a great fish to swallow up Jonah.